The

Biggest Scam

on

Earth

Disclaimer

The contents of this book are intended for informational and educational purposes only. The author has made every effort to ensure the accuracy and reliability of the information provided, but the material is provided "as is." The author and publisher do not assume and hereby disclaim any liability to any party for any loss, damage, or disruption caused by errors or omissions, whether such errors or omissions result from negligence, accident, or any other cause.

The information presented in this book is based on the author's knowledge. Tax laws, regulations, and financial practices can change over time and may vary by jurisdiction. Readers are strongly advised to consult with qualified professionals, such as tax advisors, accountants, or legal experts, to obtain the most current and accurate information regarding their specific financial and tax situations.

This book may contain opinions and interpretations of the author. These opinions are not intended to offend or harm the feelings of any individual, group, organization, or entity. The author acknowledges the diversity of perspectives on financial and tax matters and respects the right of readers to hold their own views.

NOTHING is a bigger scam than the system around middle class

Small chapters with grand knowledge

Content

PREFACE

Money stands as an inevitable aspect of modern life, impacting both individuals and businesses, shaping economic dynamics and societal structures. Yet, have you ever taken a moment to contemplate the intricacies of the tax system? Have you ever pondered the possibility of there being provisions, tactics, and methodologies that allow individuals and organizations to significantly alleviate their tax obligations, sometimes to a remarkable extent?

Welcome to "The Biggest Scam on Earth," an extensive guide that peels away the layers of the tax framework to unveil a realm where astute individuals and influential corporations navigate the intricate landscape of taxation with remarkable finesse. Within the pages of this book, we embark on a journey through the historical evolution of taxation, exploring its origins, money laundering and the societal agreements that underpin it. We delve into the motivations driving tax optimization and shed light on the strategies employed by the world's wealthiest individuals and enterprises to mitigate their tax liabilities.

It's important to clarify that this book does not advocate for tax evasion or illicit practices. Instead, it seeks to provide a nuanced comprehension of how certain individuals and corporations legally minimize their tax burdens, utilizing legal loopholes and capitalizing on the complexities of tax laws. Through real-world examples, case studies, and expert insights, we offer a glimpse into the methodologies employed by those aiming to pay the least amount of taxes while adhering to legal boundaries.

Nevertheless, it remains paramount to acknowledge that taxes play a pivotal role in funding public services, supporting infrastructure, healthcare, education, and more. Taxes form the cornerstone of governments, enabling them to maintain stability and cater to their citizens' needs. As we explore the strategies used to reduce tax obligations, we must also confront the consequences of these actions. We will examine the impact on government revenues, wealth distribution, social inequality, and the potential ramifications for emerging economies.

Moreover, this book delves into the ethical and moral considerations surrounding tax optimization and understanding the basics of money laundering. We probe the delicate balance between individual rights and societal responsibilities, raising questions about whether it's justifiable for the most affluent individuals to minimize their tax contributions. The concept of corporate social responsibility is scrutinized, and the ethical implications of various tax optimization strategies are evaluated. Ultimately, our goal is to empower readers to make informed decisions and take charge of their financial trajectories while upholding legality and ethical accountability.

Taxation constitutes a multifaceted and ever-evolving system that touches us all. By acquiring a deeper understanding of the tactics and strategies utilized by individuals and corporations to reduce their tax liabilities, we can adeptly navigate the tax landscape and make knowledgeable choices. Join us as we embark on this enlightening expedition into the realm of taxes, delving into the motivations, repercussions, and potential for ethically responsible tax optimization.

In this book, we will not only uncover the tactics embraced by the most prosperous individuals and corporations to launder their money in various situations, but we will also delve into the historical context of taxation. By grasping the origins and development of money, we attain a broader perspective on their societal role and the fundamental principles shaping the current systems.

Before formal taxation took root, societies relied on bartering and non-monetary exchanges to fulfill economic needs. However, as civilizations expanded and governments sought funding for warfare, empire expansion, and public goods provision, formal taxation emerged. We will explore the transition from feudalism and tribute systems to structured tax systems, revealing the social contracts that evolved between rulers and their subjects.

With this groundwork established, we will dive into diverse tax types, including income tax, sales tax, property tax, and more. Demystifying intricate terminology and concepts linked to taxation, we will empower readers to traverse the tax landscape with confidence.

Venturing deeper, we will uncover the realm of money laundering and the tax optimization side of the money, where individuals and corporations strategically utilize legitimate techniques to minimize their tax burdens. Through real-life illustrations and case studies, we will scrutinize how some of the globe's most successful entities use offshore tax havens and innovative accounting practices to their benefit.

Offshore tax havens have emerged as potent tools for international tax planning, capitalizing on their appealing tax advantages and financial secrecy. Our focus will be on illuminating the distinctive traits of these tax havens while delving into the potential risks and rewards linked to their utilization. Moreover, a critical examination of multinational corporations' involvement in tax optimization will ensue, dissecting their intricate frameworks and the repercussions these hold for governments and societies at large.

The avenue of creative accounting, often exploiting legal gaps, provides another avenue for tax optimization. We will meticulously explore the tactics deployed to reposition income, amplify deductions, and curtail tax liabilities. This journey will further take us into the realm of accountants and tax professionals, assessing their ethical obligations and the intricate balance between legitimate tax planning and ethically questionable maneuvers.

While comprehending the strategies underpinning tax optimization is paramount, it's equally crucial to reckon with the ripple effects of these actions. We will scrutinize their impact on government revenues and the provisioning of public services. Additionally, we will address the far-reaching implications for wealth distribution and social inequality, casting a spotlight on the potential consequences for overall economic stability and societal well-being.

Throughout our expedition, an ongoing evaluation of the moral and ethical dimensions of tax optimization will prevail. By engaging with the equilibrium between individual rights and communal duties, our aim is to provoke readers into considering the wider ramifications of their financial choices. The notion of corporate social responsibility will be thoroughly examined, encouraging readers to introspect on the morality associated with diverse tax optimization strategies.

Practical guidance and insights from experts will punctuate our discourse, guiding readers to navigate the tax and money laundering landscape astutely. From maximizing deductions and harnessing tax credits to unraveling the benefits tied to charitable contributions, our intent is to equip individuals and enterprises with the knowledge to make informed decisions, all while adhering to the boundaries of legality and ethical obligation.

As we delve deeper into the labyrinth of tax optimization intricacies and illicit funds, we extend an invitation to readers to contemplate the lawful avenues available for trimming tax burdens. Strategies for optimizing tax deductions, money laundering strategies, decoding tax credits and incentives, and leveraging the myriad legal mechanisms to curtail tax responsibilities will be laid bare. By providing tangible advice and expert insights, our aspiration is to empower individuals and businesses to make prudent choices that align with their fiscal aspirations while staying in harmony with tax regulations.

Throughout the pages of this book, real-world instances, case studies, and interviews with experts will serve as pillars bolstering our arguments, rendering tangible insights into the universe of tax optimization. By dissecting the experiences of notable entities and individuals, we endeavor to foster a profound understanding of the strategies employed and the potential outcomes these strategies might yield.

In our pursuit, we extend our acknowledgment to the ethical and moral dimensions tethered to tax optimization. While legitimate tax planning is within the bounds of legality, it becomes imperative to weigh the broader societal implications of minimizing tax contributions. Issues of fairness, societal responsibility, and the conceivable repercussions for economic progress and communal well-being will be broached.

Through maintaining a balanced perspective, we galvanize readers to explore tax optimization while remaining tethered to legality and ethical responsibility. Our goal is to cultivate enlightened decision-making, thereby empowering individuals and enterprises to seize control over their fiscal futures while honoring their commitments to society.

It's worth noting that although this book intricately examines the strategies, techniques, and legal nuances employed by some to mitigate tax burdens, adherence to tax laws is unequivocally essential. Our stance categorically rejects any form of endorsement or encouragement for unlawful activities, money laundering or tax evasion. Our purpose hinges upon unraveling the intricate facets of the tax system, dissecting the motivations propelling tax optimization, and encouraging readers to make choices imbued with awareness, all within the ethical and legal bounds.

In wrapping up, "The Biggest Scam on Earth" emerges as an all-encompassing guide, striving to enlighten and equip readers in maneuvering the intricate realm of taxation. By embarking on a voyage through the annals of tax history, dissecting the incentives driving tax optimization, scrutinizing the tactics embraced by individuals and corporations, and unearthing the ripple effects of these maneuvers, we present a panoramic perspective of the tax terrain.Money laundering, strategies employed by the wealthy. Our aim is to kindle a thoughtful analysis of the moral and ethical ramifications tied to tax optimization, to delve into legitimate avenues for reducing tax obligations, and to foster wise financial decisions aligned with individual principles and aspirations.

Accompany us on this enlightening odyssey as we unravel the intricate threads of the tax structure, probe into the motivations and repercussions of tax optimization, and empower readers to wield a responsible grip on their fiscal destinies. Together, let's navigate the labyrinthine tapestry of "The Biggest Scam on Earth" and unlock the wisdom required to make judicious choices within the dynamic realm of finance.

The Purpose of Taxes

At its core, the function of taxes is to furnish the financial means necessary for governments to fulfill their essential responsibilities: delivering public goods and services that underpin the fabric of society. These taxes represent the lifeblood of government revenue, enabling them to sustain infrastructure, provide vital healthcare and education, offer a safety net through social welfare programs, ensure public safety, and channel resources into the holistic advancement of our collective well-being.

Enter the realm of public goods – those essential offerings that defy exclusion and rivalry. These are the services and commodities accessible to all members of society, with one person's use having no bearing on their availability to others. These indispensable provisions serve as the bedrock of societal functionality and prosperity. Think of the intricate tapestry of road networks, communal parks, impregnable national defense, the ever-watchful eyes of law enforcement, the enlightening corridors of public education, the healing embrace of healthcare institutions, and the safety net of social security programs.

Amid this intricate dance of governance and societal cohesion, taxes assume the role of chief financier for these public goods and services, acting as the lifeblood that channels resources toward their maintenance. Take away this critical flow of tax revenue, and governments would be left grappling with the challenge of maintaining essential transportation infrastructure, constraining their capacity to nurture educational and healthcare systems, and struggling to uphold the shield of citizen safety.

Beyond these tangible benefits, taxes offer governments the means to confront prevailing societal challenges and propel economic growth. They serve as the financial fuel empowering governments to implement policies and initiatives aimed at reducing disparities, supporting marginalized groups, and sparking the fires of economic progress. The revenue harnessed from taxes becomes the life force behind transformative social welfare programs, uplifting those on the fringes and propelling us all toward a shared vision of advancement.

While the act of paying taxes is frequently perceived as a weighty obligation, it's paramount to grasp the fundamental role that taxes undertake in fostering the advancement and prosperity of societies. By pooling resources through the collaborative efforts of individuals and enterprises, governments can address the comprehensive needs of their communities, guaranteeing universal access to indispensable public services and goods.

Furthermore, taxes act as catalysts for nurturing a sense of societal duty and cementing the social agreement between citizens and the governing body. In return for their tax contributions, citizens rightfully anticipate that governments will handle these funds with conscientiousness and impartiality, ultimately serving the greater interests of the entire society.

It's crucial to underline that crafting a taxation system demands a delicate equilibrium between accumulating vital revenue and nurturing economic expansion. An overbearing burden of taxes has the potential to stifle the drive of both individuals and businesses, potentially impeding the creative forces of economic productivity and innovation. Hence, governments must meticulously devise tax policies and frameworks that exude fairness, transparency, and an environment conducive to sustainable economic progress.

At its core, the essence of taxation lies in provisioning the financial means essential for governments to carry out their obligations of providing public services and goods to the community. By collecting taxes, governments can channel investments into critical areas such as infrastructure, education, healthcare, social welfare initiatives, and other pivotal services that contribute to the growth and well-being of societies. Although taxes are frequently perceived as a burden, they form a cornerstone of the social contract, playing an indispensable role in upholding the functionality and evolution of our interconnected societies.

The Evolution Of Taxes

The journey of taxation spans across the tapestry of centuries, mirroring the ebb and flow of societal needs and structures that have shaped history. From the rudimentary fiscal practices of ancient civilizations to the intricate systems that navigate our modern world, the historical trajectory of taxes offers a treasure trove of wisdom into the evolution of economic and political frameworks.

In antiquity, the concept of taxation was intimately entwined with ruling powers and the gathering of tribute. Ancient realms like Mesopotamia, Egypt, and Rome imposed levies to fund military campaigns, uphold essential infrastructure, and sustain the ruling class. These initial tax systems leaned on evaluations of agricultural output, labor contributions, and the extraction of natural resources.

As societies matured, the panorama of feudalism unfolded in medieval Europe. Under its canopy, taxes were amassed by feudal lords from their subjects, in exchange for shielding and access to land. These lords, in their own turn, were accountable to higher echelons of nobility or the monarchies. Taxation during this epoch often manifested as goods or services rather than the modern notion of currency.

The dawn of strong central governments in the Renaissance and Enlightenment epochs marked a pivot in tax paradigms. Monarchs seized the reins of power and erected more structured taxation frameworks. The late 18th century ushered in profound changes through the French Revolution, introducing the concept of progressive taxation and the novel notion of levying the affluent more significantly.

The 19th century's industrial revolution ignited a seismic transformation in tax landscapes. As economies swelled and grew intricate, governments needed to amass augmented revenue to meet the burgeoning needs of their societies. This shift birthed income taxes and steered the migration from agrarian-rooted taxation to a broader foundation encompassing industrial and commercial spheres.

The 20th century marked a turning point in taxation, propelled by economic theories and geopolitical tides. The advent of the welfare state and the expansion of governmental services paved the way for social security taxes and the establishment of comprehensive tax codes. Progressive income taxation, wherein the prosperous shouldered a greater proportion of their earnings as taxes, became a cornerstone in many nations.

In the contemporary arena, globalization and technological strides have etched their mark on tax systems. The ascent of multinational corporations and the fluidity of capital flows have introduced new dimensions to taxation. Operating across borders, these corporations have ingeniously maneuvered through tax laws, minimizing their fiscal obligations. This prompted a collective response to curtail tax avoidance and build international frameworks to counteract tax evasion.

In the present day, tax systems exhibit a diverse mosaic across countries, reflecting their distinctive economic, political, and societal landscapes. Some nations lean towards consumption-based taxes like value-added taxes (VAT), while others emphasize income and corporate taxes. The ongoing evolution of tax systems remains a manifestation of changing societal needs, economic dynamics, and global currents.

Delving into the historical chronicle of taxes yields a repository of insights into the world of economic and political systems. It unfurls the interplay between governance, society, and taxation, unraveling the motivations and tribulations interwoven with the gathering of taxes. Unraveling this historical backdrop is paramount in unearthing the intricacies of contemporary tax frameworks and in addressing the ongoing dialogues enveloping taxation's role in society.

Taxation and Social Contract

Taxation and the social contract are deeply intertwined, forming the essence of the relationship between individuals and their government. This intricate web outlines the rights and duties of citizens and the reciprocal obligations of the government. Central to this intricate dance is taxation, acting as a linchpin in preserving equilibrium between individual rights and societal obligations for both citizens and governing bodies.

The crux of the social contract postulates that citizens surrender certain personal freedoms and allocate a portion of their authority to the government in exchange for safeguarded rights and the delivery of essential public goods and services. At its core, taxation becomes the conduit through which individuals contribute their equitable share to finance governmental operations and the realization of societal requisites.

Through the mechanism of taxation, governments secure the indispensable revenue to underwrite public goods like infrastructure, education, healthcare, national defense, and social welfare endeavors. These communal provisions enrich the entire populace, endowing crucial services that elevate the quality of life, ensure safety, and foster the collective well-being of citizens. By participating in the realm of taxes, individuals fulfill their role in nurturing the shared prosperity of society.

Concurrently, taxation maps out the rights and anticipations of individuals concerning the government. Citizens possess the right to comprehend the allocation of their tax dollars, to demand transparency and accountability in government expenditure, and to engage in the decision-making fabric that molds tax policies. Beyond this, they bear the right to impartial and just taxation, wherein the load is apportioned in a manner that mirrors capacity to pay and advocates for social equity.

However, achieving equilibrium between rights and responsibilities in taxation is no simple feat. Disputes emerge regarding the suitable level of taxation, the distribution of tax encumbrances, and the efficiency of government spending. These discussions mirror the ongoing dialogue between individuals and governments concerning the rightful scope and purpose of taxation in society.

Furthermore, the social contract harbors ethical considerations within the realm of
taxation. While individuals possess the right to pursue legitimate avenues to alleviate their tax burdens, they are also ethically bound to shoulder their equitable share. Ethical tax conduct entails navigating the terrain between capitalizing on valid deductions, incentives, and exemptions, while simultaneously discharging obligations to the collective.

Likewise, governments carry an ethical duty to shape tax policies that are impartial, lucid, and conducive to the well-being of all citizens. This encompasses thwarting tax evasion and circumvention, addressing vulnerabilities in the system, and ensuring that taxation nurtures economic progress, societal fairness, and sustainability.

In summation, the interplay between taxation and the social contract constitutes the bedrock of the relationship between individuals and governments. Through tax payment, citizens fulfill their responsibilities in bolstering the common good, while governments honor their commitment to offering vital public goods and services. The equilibrium of rights and responsibilities in taxation is an ongoing discourse that necessitates perpetual evaluation and adaptation to maintain a just and fair society.

Early Economic Systems

Before the advent of formal taxation, the early tapestry of human societies was woven with diverse economic systems for the exchange of goods and services. Notably, two distinct systems, bartering and non-monetary exchanges, rose to prominence, shaping the contours of early economies and casting a significant imprint on economic interactions.

Bartering, a fundamental form of exchange, entailed the direct swapping of goods or services between individuals sans the involvement of money. In the realm of barter, individuals would negotiate trades, leveraging their own resources or expertise for the items or services they required. For instance, a farmer might engage in a transaction with another farmer, exchanging harvested crops for livestock. This practice empowered individuals to meet their needs by harnessing their individual assets, fostering a spirit of self-reliance within communities.

The prevalence of bartering systems spanned early civilizations and hinged on the concept of a "double coincidence of wants." This meant that two parties had to possess goods or services that the other party sought concurrently. Navigating such alignments could be arduous and time-intensive, necessitating robust social networks and effective communication to unearth counterparts with complementary demands and resources.

To surmount the limitations inherent in bartering, non-monetary exchanges emerged as a viable alternative. These exchanges revolved around indirect modes of trade, incorporating intermediary goods or commodities that held widespread recognition and acceptance within a specific community or region. These intermediary goods, often dubbed mediums of exchange, streamlined transactions and sidestepped the need for an immediate "double coincidence of wants."

One of the earliest instances of a non-monetary exchange system involved the use of cowrie shells as a form of currency in ancient China and other corners of Asia. Owing to their distinct attributes and scarcity, cowrie shells evolved into an acknowledged medium of exchange for a variety of goods and services. Analogous illustrations of non-monetary exchanges encompassed the utilization of salt, livestock, grain, and precious metals like gold and silver as mediums of transaction.

While bartering and non-monetary exchanges functioned effectively within localized communities, they posed challenges as economic dealings expanded beyond immediate social circles. These systems lacked standardization and uniformity, rendering it intricate to gauge the relative value of diverse goods and services. The dearth of a universal unit of measurement made trade cumbersome, stifling the potential for economic expansion and specialization.

As societies burgeoned and grew intricate, the advent of standardized currencies and formal systems of taxation became a requisite to surmount the constraints of bartering and non-monetary exchanges. The inception of currencies, encompassing coins and subsequently paper money, bestowed a shared medium of exchange that streamlined trade and eased economic transactions.

The shift from bartering and non-monetary exchanges to structured taxation and monetary systems denoted a significant juncture in the trajectory of economic systems. While bartering and non-monetary exchanges undeniably played pivotal roles in nascent economies, they were progressively supplanted by more streamlined and standardized monetary systems that catalyzed the emergence of sophisticated societies and enabled trade on grander scales.

Apprehending the early economic systems of bartering and non-monetary exchanges unveils the origins of economic interactions and illuminates the gradual emergence of monetary systems. These systems acted as a prologue to the advent of taxation and the ensuing evolution of economic structures, forming the bedrock for the intricate economic frameworks that grace our contemporary world.

Feudalism and Tribute Systems

During the medieval epoch, the socio-economic tapestry was woven with the intricate threads of the feudal system and tribute systems, governing economic interactions and delineating tax responsibilities. These systems were the axis around which obligations and relationships between lords or rulers and their subjects revolved, sculpting the economic panorama and the dispersal of resources.

Feudalism, which held sway in Europe from the 9th to the 15th century, was a hierarchical framework grounded in land ownership and labor commitments. At its zenith stood monarchs or feudal lords, custodians of extensive tracts of land, who allocated portions of it to vassals, oftentimes in exchange for military service or expressions of loyalty. In reciprocation, vassals bore a spectrum of obligations, encompassing military backing, counsel, and other services bestowed upon their lord.

A linchpin of feudalism was the notion of fiefs – parcels of land bestowed by a lord upon a vassal. Vassals, in their turn, furnished labor and resources to their lords, reaping from the land they held. This labor, recognized as serfdom, typically entailed agricultural toil on the lord's property, culminating in a share of the produce or services rendered to the lord as tribute or rent.

Conversely, the tribute system, extant in various ancient civilizations, orbited around the commitments between conquered territories and their rulers. Conquered regions or subjugated communities were mandated to offer tribute, manifesting as goods, resources, or labor, to the ruling authority. This tribute affirmed allegiance and solidified the ruling power's dominion and sway over the annexed territories.

In both the annals of feudalism and the framework of tribute systems, the obligations of subjects towards their lords or rulers encompassed economic contributions that set the bedrock for taxation. Monetary exchanges were not universal or readily accessible during these eras, rendering contributions non-monetary. Subjects discharged their duties by delivering agricultural yields, labor, military aid, or other commodities and services.

These obligations were often upheld through a fusion of legal and societal mechanisms. Breaching commitments could trigger penalties, forfeiture of land, or even expulsion from the lord's safeguard, subjecting individuals to manifold vulnerabilities. In return for their contributions, subjects anticipated protection, justice, and specific entitlements from their lords or rulers.

Crucially, it's worth noting that taxation systems during the reign of feudalism and tribute systems predominantly served to sustain ruling powers and maintain societal harmony, rather than underpinning the provision of communal goods or services. The amassed resources were frequently employed by the ruling elite to support their lifestyles, finance conflicts, erect fortifications, and perpetuate their dominion.

As the curtain descended on feudalism and societies embraced more centralized governance models, particularly with the ascent of nation-states, more structured and standardized taxation systems emerged. These systems pivoted the focal point of taxation from bolstering the ruling echelon to financing comprehensive public goods and services, such as infrastructure, defense, and administration.

The feudal system and tribute systems cast profound imprints on the economic and social dynamics of their epochs. While they may appear distant from modern taxation systems, they forged the bedrock of the concept of economic commitments and taxation, which would continue to evolve with the passage of time. Scrutinizing these historical frameworks yields invaluable insights into the roots of tax responsibilities and the complex interplay between rulers and their subjects in earlier societies.

Emergence of Formal Taxation

The dawn of formal taxation marked a pivotal juncture in the landscape of government finance, particularly in terms of fueling military campaigns and facilitating the expansion of empires. As civilizations burgeoned and the clamor for resources heightened, rulers embarked on instituting methodical tax systems to amass the requisite revenue for their grand pursuits.

Across history, wars have stood as transformative forces, shaping the trajectories of nations and igniting the demand for substantial resources. In antiquity, the burdens of warfare were often borne by rulers or elites who bankrolled military ventures from personal coffers or the spoils of conquest. However, as conflicts swelled in scope and intricacy, rulers discerned the need for dependable and predictable revenue streams.

Ancient empires, such as those in Mesopotamia, Egypt, and Rome, heralded the inception of formal taxation systems to bankroll their military enterprises. These embryonic tax frameworks aimed to draw resources from their subjects, funneling the proceeds towards the expansion of their dominions. Taxes were frequently levied on agricultural yields, land holdings, commerce, and other economic pursuits that promised revenue infusion for the governing elite.

Beyond just funding warfare, formal taxation was a linchpin in sustaining and amplifying empires. Annexed territories often assimilated into the taxation fabric of the ruling power, channeling the resources and affluence of these regions back to the central authority. Taxes imposed on subjugated lands not only underwrote the empire's operations but also served as a conduit for control, solidifying the empire's hegemony.

As societies matured, tax systems acquired finesse and efficiency. The introduction of standardized currencies streamlined tax collection, enabling rulers to assess and quantify their resources more adeptly. Taxes transitioned into coinage, forging a universal medium of exchange that smoothed transactions and facilitated wealth accumulation.

At times, rulers designated tax collectors or tax farmers to manage the tax collection process on their behalf. These collectors bore the responsibility of ensuring adherence and overseeing the collection process, often receiving a percentage of the revenues as compensation. This practice endured for ages and found traction in various civilizations and empires.

The advent of formal taxation held profound ramifications for both rulers and their subjects. For rulers, it unveiled a reliable and sustainable source of revenue that could be channeled towards maintaining societal harmony, expanding territories, and projecting authority. For subjects, taxation implied contributing a slice of their prosperity or resources to the ruling authority, typically with the expectation of security and governance in return.

Nonetheless, taxation didn't uniformly enjoy a warm reception from the populace. Excessive taxation or inequitable distribution of tax burdens could kindle discontent and dissent. Throughout history, instances of tax revolts and uprisings burgeoned when individuals or factions felt shackled by onerous tax loads or when they perceived their contributions as misappropriated or diverging from the common welfare.

The advent of formal taxation as a means to underwrite wars and empire-building laid the foundation for the evolution of more comprehensive tax systems that grace modern times. While the motivations and methodologies of tax collection have morphed, the foundational objective of generating revenue for government functions remains a bedrock facet of taxation. Apprehending the historical backdrop of taxation yields insights into its origins, the interplay between rulers and subjects, and the persistent tensions that have steered the evolution of tax systems across epochs.

Basic Tax Terminology and Concepts

To skillfully navigate the realm of taxes, a firm grasp of fundamental terminology and concepts is imperative. This foundational knowledge not only facilitates comprehension of the labyrinthine tax systems but also empowers individuals to make astute decisions concerning their tax responsibilities. Here's an introduction to key tax terms and concepts that warrant your acquaintance:

Tax: A mandated financial levy or assessment imposed by the government upon individuals, businesses, or other entities, with the intention of procuring funds for public services and goods.

Taxpayer: An individual or entity accountable for fulfilling tax obligations. This encompassing category incorporates individuals, the self-employed, corporations, partnerships, and an array of organizational types.

Taxable Income: The segment of an individual's earnings or a business's profits subject to taxation, subsequent to factoring in deductions, exemptions, and allowances.

Tax Rate: The percentage at which earnings or profits are taxed. Tax rates can be progressive, escalating in tandem with ascending income or profits, or they can adopt a uniform rate, unaffected by income tiers.

Deductions: Expenses, allocations, or exemptions that pare down an individual's or business's taxable income. Common deductions encompass business costs, mortgage interest, philanthropic donations, and specific educational expenditures.

Credits: Abatements in tax liability that directly counterbalance the owed tax amount. Tax credits hinge on diverse factors, including income levels, dependent status, education-related costs, or investments promoting energy efficiency.

Filing Status: The classification of individuals for tax purposes, predicated on marital status and other considerations. Notable filing statuses encompass single, married filing jointly, married filing separately, and head of household.

Tax Return: A dossier or form tendered to tax authorities (e.g., the Internal Revenue Service in the United States) that lays out exhaustive details about an individual's or business's income, deductions, credits, and tax liability for a designated tax period.

Taxable Event: An action or incident that triggers an obligation to pay taxes. Instances of taxable events comprise earning income, selling assets, or realizing capital gains.

Tax Withholding: The mechanism whereby employers deduct a portion of an employee's remuneration to cover the estimated tax liability. This withholding modus operandi ensures that taxes are dispersed throughout the year, rather than accumulating as a lump sum during tax-filing time.

Tax Evasion: The illicit act of willfully dodging taxes by underreporting income, inflating deductions, or masking assets to elude full tax payment.

Tax Audit: A scrutiny and assessment of an individual's or business's financial records, returns, and relevant documents by tax authorities to validate the accuracy and compliance of tax submissions.

These bedrock tax terms and concepts furnish an embarkation point for acquainting yourself with the language and bedrock principles of taxation. Armed with this vocabulary, you are better positioned to decipher tax-related dialogues, decipher tax forms and guidelines, and execute judicious choices regarding your tax responsibilities.

Types of Taxes

Taxation manifests in diverse forms, each tailored to solicit revenue from distinct economic activities or origins. Comprehending these varied tax types is pivotal for individuals and businesses to adhere to tax laws and manage their financial commitments. Here are several prevalent tax categories:

Income Tax: Levied on individuals and businesses contingent upon their earnings or gains. It's typically imposed by governments on assorted income sources, including wages, salaries, self-employment income, rental income, dividends, and capital gains. Income tax rates can follow a progressive trajectory, scaling up as income levels ascend.

Sales Tax: Imposed on the purchase of goods and services. It's often computed as a percentage of the transaction amount and collected by the vendor, who then remits it to the government. Sales tax norms and rates can diverge across regions, and specific goods or services may be exempt or governed by distinct tax rates.

Property Tax: Applicable to the value of real estate, encompassing land, structures, and particular personal property types. Generally overseen by local governments, property taxes finance local amenities like schools, infrastructure, and public safety. The tax quantum hinges on the appraised property value.

Capital Gains Tax: Applied to the profit generated from selling or divesting assets like stocks, bonds, real estate, or valuable personal property. The tax calculus centers on the discrepancy between the sale price and the acquisition cost of the asset, with distinct tax rates often governing short-term and long-term capital gains.

Corporate Tax: Levied on corporate or business entity profits. The computation often centers on the company's net income post accounting for permissible deductions and exemptions. Corporate tax rates can deviate across regions, and multinational corporations might encounter additional intricacies when gauging their tax liabilities.

Excise Tax: Imposed on specific commodities or services, frequently tethered to quantity or volume sold. Instances encompass taxes on tobacco, alcohol, gasoline, luxury items, and environmentally deleterious products. Manufacturers or distributors typically collect these taxes, eventually transferring them to consumers.

Payroll Tax: Applicable to employers and employees to fund social security programs, Medicare, and other social insurance initiatives. Generally calculated as a percentage of wages or salaries, these taxes are deducted from employees' earnings by employers.

Estate Tax: Also recognized as inheritance tax, it pertains to the transfer of wealth or assets from a deceased individual to their beneficiaries. The tax calculus often takes the estate's value into account, occasionally subject to exemptions and thresholds.

Value-Added Tax (VAT): A consumption tax instituted on the value added at each juncture of goods and services production and distribution. Ubiquitous beyond the United States, VAT is predicated on the variance between sales price and production input costs.

Import and Export Duties: Acknowledged as tariffs, these taxes are imposed on goods entering or exiting a country. Crafted to shield domestic industries, regulate trade, and amplify government revenue, these duties are pivotal components of international commerce.

These exemplify merely a fraction of the myriad tax types worldwide. The precise tax types and rates vary markedly across jurisdictions.

Progressive and Regressive Tax Systems

Tax systems exhibit distinct categorizations: progressive and regressive, grounded in how the tax load aligns with income or wealth. These divergent approaches wield consequential ramifications for wealth dispersion within a society.

Progressive Tax System: In this configuration, tax rates ascend in tandem with rising income or wealth. The result is that those with higher income or greater wealth shoulder a heftier portion of their earnings or assets in taxes, vis-à-vis individuals or entities with lower income or wealth. This approach often aspires to foster an equitable distribution of the tax burden and mitigate income inequality.

By imposing a more substantial tax responsibility on the affluent, progressive tax systems aspire to foster a more pronounced redistribution of resources. The rationale driving progressive taxation is that individuals capable of contributing more ought to do so, in order to buttress public goods and services, as well as extend support to those in need. These systems often feature multiple tax brackets, each accompanied by augmented tax rates as income or wealth escalates.

Regressive Tax System: Conversely, a regressive tax system diminishes the tax burden as income or wealth augments. Under such a setup, individuals or entities with lower income shoulder a more substantial fraction of their earnings or assets in taxes, compared to those with higher income or wealth. This strategy can intensify income inequality and disproportionately impact those with limited incomes.

Regressive taxes often place a weightier load on fundamental necessities like sustenance, attire, and housing—components constituting a larger segment of the income for those with lower earnings. Instances of regressive taxes encompass sales taxes, excise taxes, and specific flat taxes that impose a uniform tax rate, irrespective of income. Such taxes can significantly affect individuals with modest incomes, consequently deepening the chasm in wealth distribution within a society.

The repercussions of progressive and regressive tax systems on wealth distribution stimulate ongoing discussions and analyses. Advocates of progressive tax systems argue that they foster fairness and social equity by rebalancing wealth and underpinning social welfare programs. Their stance is that those who have profited most from society ought to proportionately contribute toward its sustenance and well-being.

On the flip side, critics of progressive tax systems contend that they could stymie productivity and investment, given that elevated tax rates for the affluent might diminish incentives for wealth generation and economic advancement. They posit that a regressive tax system, which imposes a lighter tax burden on those with higher income or entities, might fuel entrepreneurship and investment, propelling overall economic prosperity.

For policymakers, attaining an optimum equilibrium in tax systems presents a multifaceted challenge. It mandates weighing social and economic considerations, as well as the broader objectives of wealth distribution, economic expansion, and societal welfare. Ultimately, the architecture and application of tax systems should strive to strike a harmony between stimulating economic growth and mitigating income inequality, while taking into account the distinctive attributes and requisites of each society.

The Motivations Behind Tax Optimization

Reputation and Public Perception: The reputation of individuals and businesses can be influenced by their tax practices. Some entities choose to engage in transparent and responsible tax optimization strategies to maintain a positive image and public trust. By adhering to ethical tax practices, they aim to avoid negative public perceptions, legal controversies, or potential damage to their brand reputation.

Business Strategy and Growth: Tax optimization can also be integrated into broader business strategies and growth plans. Companies may strategically structure their operations, investments, and international activities to minimize tax liabilities and create a competitive advantage. Optimizing taxes can provide additional resources for business expansion, innovation, and diversification.

Legal Risk Mitigation: Engaging in tax optimization within the boundaries of the law can help mitigate legal risks associated with tax avoidance or evasion. By following established tax planning principles and guidelines, individuals and businesses can minimize the risk of facing legal challenges, penalties, or audits from tax authorities.

Government Incentives and Stimulus: Governments often provide incentives, deductions, and credits to encourage specific behaviors, such as investments in renewable energy, research and development, or affordable housing. Individuals and businesses may engage in tax optimization to take advantage of these government-sponsored initiatives, thereby contributing to societal goals while optimizing their tax positions.

Overall Financial Planning: Tax optimization is often integrated into broader financial planning strategies. Individuals may consider their tax implications when making decisions about retirement planning, education funding, charitable giving, and other financial goals. By optimizing taxes as part of comprehensive financial planning, individuals aim to achieve their long-term financial objectives more effectively.

Tax optimization strategies are legal and commonly employed, engaging in aggressive tax avoidance schemes that violate the intent of the law or involve fraudulent practices can lead to legal consequences and reputational damage.

Legal vs. Illegal Tax Evasion

Tax evasion refers to the illegal act of intentionally evading the payment of taxes by deliberately misrepresenting or concealing income, assets, or transactions to reduce one's tax liability. It is important to distinguish between legal tax optimization strategies, which aim to minimize tax burdens within the confines of the law, and illegal tax evasion, which involves fraudulent or deceptive practices to unlawfully evade taxes.

Understanding the boundary between legal and illegal tax evasion is crucial for individuals and businesses to maintain compliance with tax laws. Here are key points to consider:

Compliance with Tax Laws: Legal tax optimization strategies operate within the framework of tax laws and regulations. They involve understanding and utilizing available deductions, exemptions, credits, and incentives to minimize tax liabilities. Tax planning within legal boundaries is an accepted practice and an essential part of financial management.

Purpose and Intent: The key differentiating factor between legal tax optimization and illegal tax evasion is the purpose and intent behind the actions. Legal tax optimization aims to legitimately reduce tax liabilities by making use of tax provisions and incentives. In contrast, illegal tax evasion involves intentionally concealing income, inflating deductions, or engaging in fraudulent schemes to evade taxes unlawfully.

Transparency and Accuracy: Legal tax optimization strategies prioritize transparency and accurate reporting of income, expenses, and transactions. Individuals and businesses engaging in tax planning should maintain accurate records and disclose information truthfully and completely. In contrast, tax evasion involves intentionally providing false or misleading information to tax authorities.

Professional Advice and Expertise: Legal tax optimization often involves seeking advice from tax professionals, such as accountants or tax advisors, who provide guidance on legitimate tax-saving strategies. Tax professionals help individuals and businesses navigate complex tax laws, identify eligible deductions, and ensure compliance. However, tax professionals must uphold ethical standards and refrain from promoting or engaging in illegal tax evasion practices.

Use of Legal Loopholes: Legal tax optimization may involve taking advantage of legal loopholes or gray areas in tax laws. These loopholes refer to unintended gaps or inconsistencies in the tax legislation that can be exploited within the boundaries of the law. While using legal loopholes is permissible, engaging in activities solely for the purpose of exploiting these loopholes without a genuine economic purpose may be considered abusive and could attract scrutiny from tax authorities.

Penalties and Consequences: Engaging in illegal tax evasion can have severe legal and financial consequences. Tax authorities have the power to investigate suspected cases of tax evasion, impose fines, seize assets, and pursue criminal charges. The penalties for tax evasion vary across jurisdictions but can include substantial fines, imprisonment, reputational damage, and legal liabilities.Now let's read the most important lessons of the book in the next two chapters

Strategies Employed by Wealthy

The practice of utilizing offshore tax havens and intricate corporate setups has been a common approach for affluent individuals and companies to effectively reduce their tax obligations. This approach involves forming entities in regions with favorable tax regulations, enabling them to curtail or avoid taxes. One notable example involves the utilization of offshore accounts and shell corporations.

In this scenario, a prosperous individual or business entity might establish an offshore account in a jurisdiction with lower tax rates. Subsequently, funds or assets are stored within this offshore account, ensuring a certain level of confidentiality and potentially leading to decreased tax responsibilities. By directing income or profits through this offshore account, the individual or corporation can capitalize on the more advantageous tax rates or exemptions available in that specific jurisdiction.

Similarly, shell corporations, typically registered in areas with lax corporate regulations, can be employed to minimize tax liabilities. These entities often lack substantial operational activities and primarily serve as vehicles for holding assets or executing financial transactions. By channeling income or profits through a shell company, the individual or corporation could potentially reduce tax obligations by exploiting loopholes or evading tax reporting obligations.

For instance, consider a company 'X' based in the US aiming to minimize tax on their earnings. They establish a company 'Y' in a tax haven like the Cayman Islands. Company Y strategically possesses the intellectual property necessary for company X's operations. Y then licenses this IP to X. Although X generates $50B post expenses, they seek to avoid taxes. Given that Y is still owed for IP licensing, X must pay Y for this service. Y bills $50B for leasing their IP to X. As a result, X's profit becomes $0, leading to a 0% tax liability. Company Y's profit now stands at $50B, subject to a zero tax rate in the Cayman Islands, effectively evading taxes. It's important to note that X and Y are essentially the same collaborative entity, just functioning as separate units.

Transfer Pricing and Manipulation of Intellectual Property Rights

Another tactic deployed by multinational corporations involves manipulating transfer pricing and intellectual property rights. Transfer pricing pertains to setting prices for goods, services, or intangible assets exchanged among different subsidiaries within a single multinational corporation. Through manipulating these prices, corporations can shift profits to jurisdictions with lower tax rates, ultimately decreasing their overall tax burden.

For example, a multinational corporation might allocate a substantial portion of its intellectual property rights, such as patents or trademarks, to a subsidiary in a jurisdiction with low taxes. This subsidiary can then levy considerable royalties or licensing charges to other entities within the corporation utilizing the intellectual property. This maneuver effectively moves profits to the jurisdiction with lower tax rates, leading to reduced taxation for the corporation as a whole.

Tax Inversions and Corporate Mergers

Tax inversions entail multinational corporations restructuring their operations to change their tax residency from a higher-tax jurisdiction to a lower-tax one. This strategy is usually executed through corporate mergers or acquisitions involving companies based in countries with more favorable tax environments.

In a tax inversion, a multinational corporation headquartered in a high-tax jurisdiction merges with or acquires a company located in a low-tax jurisdiction. Through this merger or acquisition, the corporation shifts its tax residency to the lower-tax jurisdiction, potentially resulting in substantial tax savings. This approach permits corporations to make the most of lower tax rates, access tax incentives, and optimize their global tax positions.

These examples highlight some of the methods employed by affluent individuals and corporations to diminish their tax liabilities.

Although these methods might be lawful, they have been subject to scrutiny and critique due to concerns about their influence on equitable taxation and income inequality. Efforts have been undertaken by governments and international organizations to address these practices and close loopholes, ensuring that tax systems are fair and conducive to sustainable economic growth.

Tax Havens and their characteristics

Tax havens, also referred to as offshore financial centers or international financial hubs, represent jurisdictions that provide attractive tax and regulatory landscapes for individuals and companies aiming to curtail their tax obligations.

These havens lure entities with enticing features, including low or even non-existent tax rates, stringent confidentiality statutes, minimal requirements for financial reporting, and an array of incentives. Here's an insight into tax havens and their core characteristics:

Minimal or Zero Taxation: Tax havens generally present substantially lower tax rates compared to other regions. Certain havens even impose nominal or zero taxes on specific forms of income, such as corporate profits, capital gains, dividends, or interest earnings. These advantageous tax rates magnetize individuals and enterprises seeking to alleviate their tax burdens.

Privacy and Confidentiality: Confidentiality laws in tax havens are often rigorous, safeguarding the privacy of entities and individuals. They enforce stringent regulations governing the divulgence of financial data, rendering it arduous for tax authorities from external jurisdictions to access or procure information regarding financial transactions or assets held within the tax haven.

Opacity: Tax havens usually necessitate minimal mandates for financial reporting and may abstain from partaking in international endeavors striving for transparency and the combat of tax evasion, such as the Common Reporting Standard (CRS) or the Exchange of Information for Tax Purposes (EOI). This opaqueness can impede tax authorities in other jurisdictions from identifying or tracing funds within tax havens.

Insufficient Substantial Economic Presence: Tax havens might be known for hosting entities with negligible or even no substantive economic activity. These jurisdictions offer an environment where corporations can be established with minimal physical presence, workforce, or economic substance, allowing them to leverage tax benefits without engaging in significant business undertakings.

Tax Benefits and Specialized Economic Zones: Tax havens often extend an array of tax benefits and specialized economic zones to allure businesses and individuals. These enticements encompass tax breaks, exemptions, or reduced rates tailored for specific industries, activities, or types of income. Within tax havens, specialized economic zones could confer extra advantages such as exemptions from customs duties, streamlined regulations, or propitious investment terms.

Inadequate Regulatory Oversight: Tax havens may enforce less stringent regulations and oversight when compared to other jurisdictions. This could breed an environment conducive to illicit financial activities, money laundering, and tax evasion. Nevertheless, many tax havens have initiated measures to bolster their regulatory frameworks, aligning them with international standards and battling illicit financial flows.

Access to Global Financial Services: Financial havens commonly extend a broad spectrum of financial services, encompassing banking, asset management, insurance, and trust services. These jurisdictions captivate individuals and corporations seeking sophisticated financial services coupled with tax benefits.

Not all jurisdictions classified as tax havens partake in illicit activities or facilitate tax evasion. Some jurisdictions might extend favorable tax frameworks to draw legitimate enterprises, foreign investments, and economic development.

Nevertheless, the aura of secrecy and scant transparency linked to certain tax havens has raised apprehensions about their implications for global tax systems, equity, and income disparity.

Famous Offshore Tax Havens

Numerous jurisdictions across the globe have gained renown as offshore tax havens due to their advantageous tax and regulatory landscapes. While these havens provide certain advantages for individuals and businesses aiming to optimize their tax liabilities, they are accompanied by associated risks and ethical deliberations. Let's delve into some prominent offshore tax havens, outlining their benefits:

Cayman Islands:

• Absence of corporate income tax, capital gains tax, and direct taxes on individuals.
• Robust financial services sector encompassing banking, funds, and insurance.
• High level of confidentiality coupled with minimal reporting requisites.

Switzerland:

• Robust banking secrecy and privacy regulations.
• Alluring financial services, including wealth management and private banking.
• Political stability alongside well-developed infrastructure.

Panama:

- Favorable tax framework with exemptions on offshore-derived income.
- Robust asset protection legislation.
- Utilization of bearer shares to ensure anonymity and privacy.

British Virgin Islands (BVI):

- No corporate income tax, capital gains tax, or inheritance tax.
- Sparse reporting requisites accompanied by a high level of confidentiality.
- Simplified company establishment and administration processes.

Luxembourg:

- Alluring tax incentives for corporations and investment funds.
- Robust financial sector encompassing banking and fund management.
- Extensive network of double taxation treaties.

Bermuda:

- Absence of corporate income tax, capital gains tax, and value-added tax.
- Vibrant insurance and reinsurance industry.

• Sparse reporting requisites accompanied by confidentiality.

The advantages tied to offshore tax havens can fluctuate based on individual business activities, and shifts in regulations. While tax optimization is a legitimate objective, it is imperative to weigh the plausible legal ramifications of resorting to tax havens..

The Role of Multinational
Corporations

Multinational corporations wield a significant influence within the landscape of tax optimization, capitalizing on their global operations to structure their activities in ways that minimize their worldwide tax liabilities.

While some tax optimization strategies are legally aligned with business objectives, others have faced intense scrutiny due to perceived ethical implications and potential repercussions on public revenues. Let's delve into an overview of the multifaceted role played by multinational companies in the realm of tax optimization:

Global Operations: Multinational companies possess the unique capability to operate across multiple countries, each with distinct tax rates, incentives, and regulations. This enables them to design their operations in a manner that allocates income, expenses, and profits across various jurisdictions, ultimately optimizing their overall tax responsibility.

Transfer Pricing: A prevalent tax optimization strategy utilized by multinational corporations is transfer pricing. This tactic involves setting prices for transactions between affiliated entities under the same corporate umbrella. By strategically adjusting transfer prices, corporations can maneuver profits to jurisdictions featuring lower tax rates, thereby diminishing their tax burden.

Holding Companies: Frequently, multinational corporations establish holding companies in jurisdictions offering favorable tax frameworks. These holding companies can be tasked with managing intellectual property, overseeing royalties, and conducting other financial activities. As a result, the corporation benefits from reduced tax rates applied to income derived from these ventures.

Tax Inversions: Some multinational entities engage in tax inversions, which entail the restructuring of their operations to alter their tax residency from a higher-tax jurisdiction to one with more advantageous tax conditions. This transformation might involve mergers or acquisitions with companies hailing from countries boasting favorable tax environments.

Base Erosion and Profit Shifting (BEPS): BEPS encapsulates the strategies employed by multinational corporations to artificially redirect profits from higher-tax jurisdictions to lower-tax jurisdictions, thus curtailing their overall tax liability. This phenomenon has prompted international endeavors, spearheaded by the OECD, aimed at tackling and curbing such practices.

Double Taxation Treaties: Multinational corporations can leverage the double taxation treaties established between countries to mitigate the repercussions of facing taxation twice on the same income. Such treaties often provide mechanisms, such as tax credits or exemptions, to circumvent excessive taxation.

Ethical Considerations: The role of multinational companies in tax optimization has given rise to ethical quandaries. Critics contend that aggressive tax optimization tactics can deplete the tax foundation of countries, depriving them of vital revenue earmarked for public services. A debate ensues over whether these practices contribute to the escalation of income inequality and social disparities.

Legal and Regulatory Scrutiny: Governments worldwide are progressively intensifying their oversight of the tax practices adopted by multinational corporations. Many jurisdictions have introduced or reinforced regulations designed to counteract aggressive tax optimization and ensure that corporations fulfill their due contributions of taxes.

In essence, the engagement of multinational corporations in tax optimization is a multifaceted realm, marked by intricate strategies, evolving ethical discourse, and heightened regulatory attention. While these corporations seek to align with legal parameters and business goals, the broader societal ramifications of their tax practices continue to prompt discussions and actions aimed at fostering transparency, fairness, and equitable fiscal contributions.

Tax Planning vs. Tax Avoidance

Tax planning and tax avoidance are terms frequently discussed in the context of managing tax obligations, yet they encompass distinct approaches with varying ethical and legal implications. Although both involve strategic efforts to reduce taxes, their intent, methodologies, and outcomes distinguish them. Let's delve into the distinction between tax planning and tax avoidance:

Tax Planning:

Definition: Tax planning entails the lawful and permissible process of organizing one's financial affairs to capitalize on available deductions, credits, exemptions, and incentives outlined within the scope of tax laws.

Intent: The primary objective of tax planning is to minimize tax liabilities while adhering to the spirit and specifics of tax laws. It necessitates meticulous assessment of one's financial status and activities to strategically optimize tax outcomes.

Legality: Tax planning strategies are entirely legal and authorized by tax authorities. Taxpayers possess the right to structure their matters in a manner that is most favorable from a tax standpoint, as long as they abide by the rules and mandates stipulated by tax authorities.

Transparency: Tax planning maintains transparency and refrains from concealing income, resorting to deceptive tactics, or evading tax responsibilities. Taxpayers reveal their financial particulars and leverage legitimate avenues to manage their tax burdens.

Examples: Contributing to retirement accounts, employing tax-efficient investment instruments, leveraging permissible deductions, and formulating strategies for charitable contributions exemplify legitimate tax planning methods.

Tax Avoidance:

Definition: Tax avoidance involves employing legal strategies to capitalize on loopholes, ambiguities, or inconsistencies in tax laws with the goal of minimizing tax liabilities beyond the intended scope of the law.

Intent: The primary aim of tax avoidance is to pay the least possible tax while technically adhering to the legal framework. This might encompass pushing the boundaries of the law to secure tax advantages that weren't necessarily envisaged by legislators.

Legality: While tax avoidance tactics do not entail illegal conduct, they often test the ethical fabric of tax laws and could invite regulatory and legal examination if deemed aggressive or exploitative.

Transparency: Tax avoidance may involve intricate structures, transactions, or arrangements that obscure the genuine economic essence of activities, making it challenging for tax authorities to ascertain the true nature of the proceedings. This absence of transparency sets it apart from tax planning.

Examples: Aggressively manipulating transfer pricing, artificially relocating profits, and constructing intricate corporate frameworks to harness tax loopholes are instances of tax avoidance strategies.

The essential distinction between tax planning and tax avoidance lies in their motives, legality, transparency, and ethical considerations. Tax planning centers on legally optimizing tax obligations within the confines of the law, while tax avoidance may entail capitalizing on technicalities to garner tax advantages that could be seen as ethically contentious or not in harmony with the intended rationale of tax laws.

Tax Avoidance Techniques

Tax avoidance involves employing strategic and legal methods to curtail tax obligations. While certain tax avoidance strategies align with ethical and legal parameters, others may be considered aggressive or exploitative. Here are several common tax avoidance techniques embraced by both individuals and businesses:

Income Shifting: This approach entails relocating income from a jurisdiction with higher taxes to one with lower taxes. Multinational corporations, for instance, might channel profits to subsidiaries situated in countries boasting lower tax rates, thereby diminishing their overall tax responsibility. Similarly, individuals could transfer assets or investments to family members residing in tax brackets with lower rates to capitalize on reduced tax liabilities.

Transfer Pricing: Multinational corporations adopt transfer pricing to determine prices for transactions conducted between related entities. By artificially inflating or deflating the prices of goods or services exchanged among subsidiaries, companies can maneuver profits to jurisdictions characterized by lower tax rates.

Exploitation of Deductions and Credits: Legitimate tax deductions and credits are designed to incentivize specific behaviors, such as charitable contributions or investment in particular industries. However, aggressive tax avoidance might involve capitalizing on these provisions beyond their intended scope to curtail taxable income.

Hybrid Mismatches: These mismatches result from inconsistencies in tax laws across jurisdictions, allowing entities to capitalize on differences in tax treatment. For instance, a financial instrument might be classified as debt in one country and equity in another, permitting companies to exploit resultant tax disparities.

Utilization of Tax Havens: Tax havens offer minimal or zero tax rates, confidentiality, and lenient regulations. Multinational corporations might establish subsidiaries in tax havens to manage intellectual property or conduct financial transactions, leading to diminished tax burdens.

Leveraging Double Taxation Treaties: Although these treaties aim to prevent dual taxation, they can also be exploited. Companies may route investments through countries featuring favorable tax treaties to decrease withholding taxes imposed on dividends, interest, or royalties.

Generation of Artificial Losses: Corporations could create simulated losses through intricate financial transactions, offsetting their profits and reducing their tax liability.

Conversion of Income: Certain entities might convert taxable income into capital gains, which often face lower tax rates. This may involve transforming ordinary income into gains originating from asset sales.

Payments in the Form of Leases and Royalties: Entities might structure transactions as payments for leases or royalties, enabling them to relocate profits to jurisdictions boasting lower taxes. This technique is commonly applied to transactions involving intellectual property rights.

Deductions for Debt and Interest: Borrowing funds to finance activities can allow corporations to deduct interest expenditures from their taxable income, thereby decreasing their tax liability.

Creation of Shell Companies: Establishing shell companies with minimal or no substantive business operations in jurisdictions featuring favorable tax regulations can be employed to channel funds and mitigate tax payments.

Money Laundering

Now that we have understood tax breaking successfully, Let me teach you a new chapter of your life, Money Laundering .Typically, the process of money laundeirng involves three main stages: placement, layering, and integration. In the placement stage, the criminal introduces the illicit funds into the financial system. This can be done by breaking down large sums of money into smaller amounts to avoid suspicion, and then depositing or transferring them into various accounts. This initial step helps distance the money from its criminal origins.

Let me tell you the story of Zhenli Ye Gon. He was no ordinary businessman; he was a mastermind of money laundering. Zhenli was a man of cunning and audacity, and he devised a scheme so elaborate that it would boggle the minds of even the most seasoned investigators.

Zhenli's journey into money laundering began with a pharmaceutical company. He used this legitimate front to import vast quantities of pseudoephedrine, a key ingredient in the production of methamphetamine. But here's where the real magic happened. Instead of using his ill-gotten drug proceeds directly, he funneled them into a complex web of international bank accounts, shell companies, and offshore havens.

To fully understand the story of Zhenli Ye Gon. This chapter unveils the origins of illicit funds that set the stage for a cascade of events. The introduction of these tainted assets marks the inception of a journey that weaves through shadows and deception, leaving a trail of moral ambiguity and legal complexity.

The journey begins with the birth of criminal enterprises, where individuals embrace illegal activities such as drug trafficking, corruption, or fraud. These activities yield substantial profits that beg to be concealed, thrusting the perpetrators into the realm of money laundering.

As criminal operations thrive, the funds generated bear the mark of their illicit origins. Large sums of cash emerge from the shadows, seeking to infiltrate the legitimate financial world. This newfound wealth beckons for a transformation – a laundering process that will blur the lines between legality and crime.

The realization dawns that openly using or depositing these ill-gotten gains would raise red flags. The need to cleanse the funds becomes evident, giving rise to the concept of money laundering – the art of camouflaging the origins of dirty money through a series of strategic maneuvers.

This section explores the various entry points criminals employ to introduce illicit funds into the financial system. From physical cash deposits to sophisticated electronic transfers, the methods used are as diverse as they are inventive. Bulk cash smuggling, digital transfers, and engaging intermediaries become the conduits for the funds' integration.

A key strategy for introducing illicit funds involves the creation of shell companies – entities that exist primarily on paper and have no substantial operations. These entities provide the perfect disguise for channeling dirty money into the legitimate economy, obscuring its origins and introducing a layer of complexity.

As technology evolves, so do the methods of introducing illicit funds. Cryptocurrencies emerge as a popular choice for criminals seeking anonymity and an alternate channel for money movement. This section explores the utilization of digital currencies as vehicles for introducing dirty money into the financial ecosystem.

The globalized world offers both challenges and opportunities for criminals. Crossing international borders with illicit funds requires strategic planning – the choice of favorable jurisdictions, the utilization of financial loopholes, and the understanding of the legal hurdles that may lie ahead.

Amidst the cloak of secrecy, the criminal seeks ways to introduce tainted funds into activities that are outwardly legitimate. The chapter concludes by highlighting how the introduction of illicit wealth sets the stage for the subsequent stages of money laundering –

layering and integration – as the intricate dance between legality and criminality continues.

Smurfing or Structuring

One of the earliest and most crucial steps taken by criminals to cloak their illicit gains is known as "smurfing" or "structuring." This method revolves around the subtle art of breaking down large sums of money into smaller, inconspicuous amounts, thereby evading detection and suspicion from financial authorities. Like shadows that disperse in the dark, these divided funds seem harmless when viewed individually, but collectively, they create a veil of anonymity that conceals the true magnitude and sinister origins of the wealth.

Picture a criminal with a substantial amount of dirty money earned through illicit activities such as drug trafficking or corruption. The sheer bulk of this money raises alarms in the financial world, prompting scrutiny from banks and law enforcement agencies. To evade this vigilant gaze, the criminal enacts a strategy reminiscent of a puzzle master. They begin by fragmenting the large sum into a multitude of smaller transactions, each of which falls below the reporting threshold set by financial institutions.

You all know Bernard Mandoff but you should know how Mandoff used structuring. Madoff's scheme revolved around a technique known as "structuring" or "smurfing." Instead of moving large sums of money in one fell swoop, which would raise red flags, he employed a clever strategy. Madoff had a network of associates, often family members and close friends, who conducted thousands of small transactions on his behalf. Each transaction was carefully designed to stay below reporting thresholds, making detection nearly impossible.

This process of division might involve depositing the funds into different bank accounts, transferring them between various individuals, or even using the money to make seemingly innocent purchases. The goal is to distribute the money widely, preventing any single transaction from arousing suspicion. This intricate dance of monetary dispersion requires meticulous planning, as the criminal orchestrates a symphony of transactions that will ultimately make their ill-gotten gains virtually untraceable.

The term "smurfing" derives its name from the small, blue fictional characters known for their teamwork. Similarly, in the criminal world, smurfing involves a network of individuals collaborating to conduct these multiple transactions. Each smurf, or participant, is tasked with carrying out transactions that, on their own, seem trivial, but collectively obscure the origin and intent of the funds. By blending legitimate transactions with these fragmented movements of money, the criminal achieves a sense of normalcy that shrouds their nefarious actions.

Despite the criminals' intricate efforts, financial institutions and authorities have developed mechanisms to detect and combat smurfing. Suspicious transaction reports, transaction monitoring, and regulatory compliance measures all contribute to identifying these fragmented financial movements that aim to deceive. While smurfing may appear as an effective means of hiding illicit gains, the persistent advancements in financial oversight serve as a reminder that the shadows, however deep, are never entirely impenetrable.

Cash Transactions

In money laundering, where secrecy reigns supreme, cash transactions emerge as a favored avenue for criminals to mask the origins of their ill-gotten gains. Like whispers in a crowded room, these physical exchanges of currency occur under the radar, evading the digital footprints that modern financial systems leave behind. With a discreet elegance, cash transactions offer criminals a way to introduce their tainted funds into the legitimate economy, all while avoiding the prying eyes of regulators and law enforcement agencies.

Imagine a criminal clutching a briefcase filled with stacks of currency earned through illegal activities such as drug trafficking or embezzlement. This tangible wealth is the embodiment of their illicit endeavors, and yet, it is fraught with risk in the modern financial landscape. In response, the criminal turns to cash transactions as a method to cloak their origins and intentions.

Jordan Belfort: Also known as the "Wolf of Wall Street," Belfort was convicted of securities fraud and money laundering related to his stock market manipulation schemes.
Jordan Belfort's modus operandi was simple yet effective. He encouraged his brokers and traders to conduct business primarily in cash. This cash-based approach helped Belfort avoid the scrutiny of banks and financial institutions that typically monitor electronic transactions for signs of money laundering.

Cash transactions encompass a variety of activities, from straightforward cash deposits into bank accounts to physical exchanges in high-stakes business dealings. These transactions hold an air of simplicity, as the transfer of tangible currency creates an immediate transfer of value, often beyond the reach of electronic surveillance. Banks, which extensively monitor digital transactions, find it more challenging to scrutinize the movement of cash once it enters the physical realm.

The allure of cash transactions lies in their ability to create an appearance of legitimacy. A criminal may funnel their tainted funds into businesses through cash payments, blending their ill-gotten gains with the lawful profits of the enterprise. Real estate transactions, luxury item purchases, and even charitable donations are other areas where cash transactions can seamlessly inject tainted wealth, creating a veneer of legality that obscures the true nature of the funds.

However, this method is not without its risks. The physical nature of cash leaves behind traces that can be discovered through meticulous investigation. Authorities often deploy techniques like surveillance, tracking serial numbers on banknotes, and analyzing patterns of large cash transactions to uncover money laundering schemes hidden within the folds of currency. Additionally, the bulkiness of cash can be a logistical challenge for criminals, necessitating storage, transportation, and conversion into assets that can be easily integrated into the legitimate economy.

Placement through Third Parties

In the intricate dance of money laundering, the involvement of third parties emerges as a strategic maneuver to introduce illicit funds into the financial system while deflecting suspicion from their true source. Like puppeteers orchestrating a clandestine ballet, criminals enlist the unwitting assistance of friends, family members, or employees to execute transactions that cloak the tainted origins of their wealth. This intricate web of complicity weaves a veil of trust, making it increasingly challenging for authorities to trace the illicit path of the funds.

Visualize a criminal seeking to disassociate themselves from their ill-gotten gains, as they consider the high-risk endeavor of directly introducing tainted funds into the financial system. Instead, they turn to those in their inner circle, individuals who may be unaware of the criminal origins of the funds they are asked to manage.

This elaborate charade involves using the identities and accounts of third parties to perform financial transactions on behalf of the criminal. The funds change hands through a series of transactions that give the appearance of legitimate business activities. For example, a family member might be directed to deposit the funds into their own bank account, followed by seemingly normal transactions like payments for goods or services.

By inserting this buffer of trust, criminals create a layer of plausible deniability. The family member, friend, or employee executing the transactions becomes an unwitting pawn in the money laundering scheme, unaware that they are facilitating the transformation of illicit wealth into seemingly legitimate assets.

The use of third parties allows criminals to bypass the initial stages of money laundering, such as placement and layering, with greater ease. These intermediaries often hold genuine bank accounts, reside in different jurisdictions, and appear to be engaging in routine financial activities. As a result, the transactions attract less suspicion from financial institutions and regulatory bodies.

However, this method carries its own set of risks. The third parties involved may inadvertently become embroiled in criminal activity, leading to legal repercussions for them. Additionally, financial institutions have implemented measures to identify transactions involving third parties who may be used to launder money. Banks and authorities have a responsibility to ensure that transactions are not being used to facilitate illegal activities.

As law enforcement agencies and financial institutions tighten their grip on combating money laundering, criminals must tread carefully when utilizing third parties. While this strategy can add a layer of complexity to their schemes, it is not impervious to scrutiny. The dance of placement through third parties continues, a delicate choreography where the innocent unknowingly partake in a performance orchestrated by those operating in the shadows.

Shell Companies and Offshore Accounts

The utilization of shell companies and offshore accounts stands as a pillar of sophistication, allowing criminals to sculpt an intricate illusion of legitimacy for their illicit funds. Like architects constructing a facade of normalcy, criminals establish shell companies – entities with nominal or no legitimate business activities – and offshore accounts in jurisdictions known for their lax financial regulations.

This strategic amalgamation of legal constructs weaves a tapestry of complexity that shrouds the origins of tainted wealth, enabling criminals to navigate the murky waters of the financial world undetected.

Picture a criminal surveying their ill-gotten gains, contemplating the intricate path they must traverse to legitimize their wealth. This journey often begins with the establishment of shell companies, paper entities that exist solely on documents. These companies have no operational purpose, serving as mere vessels through which funds can flow discreetly.

The criminals set up these entities in jurisdictions known for their favorable tax laws, secrecy provisions, and minimal regulatory oversight – often referred to as tax havens or offshore financial centers. These jurisdictions offer the perfect cloak of anonymity, as ownership and financial transactions related to these shell companies are shielded from prying eyes.

Once the shell companies are in place, the criminals ingeniously route their tainted funds through a maze of transactions. Funds are funneled into these companies, often through a series of intermediaries, making the initial source of the money difficult to trace. From there, the labyrinthine journey continues as funds are transferred between accounts, sometimes crossing multiple borders, before being reintroduced as seemingly legitimate assets.

Allen Stanford: A financier who was convicted of operating a Ponzi scheme and engaging in money laundering.Stanford established a network of shell companies, many of which were registered in offshore jurisdictions known for their strict bank secrecy laws and lenient financial regulations. These shell companies served as the front for his fraudulent activities, allowing him to obscure the true nature of the transactions.

The offshore accounts play a pivotal role in this intricate dance. Criminals utilize these accounts to create further layers of complexity, separating their illicit wealth from their real identities. The funds can be held in various currencies and financial instruments, providing options for diversification that mirror legitimate financial activities.

While the use of shell companies and offshore accounts offers an aura of invincibility, cracks in this façade are beginning to show.

International efforts to combat money laundering and improve transparency have prompted many jurisdictions to enhance their regulatory frameworks, making it increasingly difficult to hide behind the veil of anonymity that offshore accounts once offered.

Regulators and financial institutions are working together to implement due diligence measures that scrutinize the activities of shell companies and monitor cross-border transactions. They aim to pierce the opacity of these structures, shining a light on the mechanisms that criminals rely on to obscure the origins of their funds.

Real Estate Purchases

This chapter delves into the captivating world where criminals transform ill-gotten gains into tangible assets that stand as testaments to their financial prowess. Yet, beneath the surface allure, the real estate market becomes a battleground of deception, as criminals seek to legitimize their wealth through opulent acquisitions while concealing the origins of their funds in the intricate folds of property ownership.

As the journey of money laundering unfolds, criminals find themselves drawn to the realm of real estate. The lure of tangible assets, grand mansions, luxurious penthouses, and sprawling estates beckons, promising to translate hidden wealth into visible symbols of success. These properties stand as silent witnesses to the lengths criminals are willing to go to legitimize their gains, as they navigate a sea of financial complexities to establish ownership without revealing the secrets hidden within the foundations.

Viktor Bout, the Russian arms dealer, used real estate in money laundering by investing in luxury properties in various countries. He purchased high-value properties with the proceeds from illegal arms sales and then sold or leased them, effectively legitimizing the illicit funds and making it challenging for authorities to trace the money back to its criminal origin. These real estate transactions allowed him to launder large sums of money while maintaining a veneer of legitimacy.

Real estate purchases offer criminals the opportunity to blur the lines between legality and criminality. With each property acquisition, they immerse themselves in a complex dance of obscured ownership. Through intricate webs of shell companies, trusts, and nominees, criminals craft a veil of confusion that conceals their true identities and the origins of their funds. These arrangements, designed to deflect scrutiny, challenge investigators as they attempt to peel back the layers shrouding ownership.

Across international borders, criminals traverse the real estate landscapes of diverse countries. From opulent urban centers to tranquil countryside retreats, they purchase properties with the goal of integrating their illicit wealth into the legitimate economy. The global nature of these transactions provides criminals with the means to diversify their holdings, shielding their assets from the prying eyes of domestic authorities.

For criminals, real estate is not just about ownership; it's about investment. The properties they acquire serve dual purposes – as symbols of their newfound legitimacy and vehicles for future financial maneuvering. Criminals can launder funds by buying properties under market value, artificially inflating prices, or reselling at substantial gains, all the while obscuring the true nature of their transactions beneath the cloak of real estate's complexity.

The real estate sector is increasingly coming under scrutiny. Governments and financial institutions are implementing rigorous anti-money laundering (AML) regulations that cast a spotlight on real estate transactions. This pressure forces criminals to adapt their tactics, seeking new avenues to exploit while regulators close in on their deceptive practices.

The legacy of real estate purchases in the realm of money laundering is one of dualities – of opulence and secrecy, visibility and concealment. As investigators strive to unravel the intricate layers of ownership, the chapter concludes with the realization that while real estate remains a potent tool for criminals seeking to legitimize their wealth, it also represents a battleground where the boundaries between illusion and truth are relentlessly tested.

Trade Money Laundering

A method that criminals employ to cloak the origins of their illicit funds within the legitimate trade of goods and services. A captivating blend of commerce and criminality, this practice involves manipulating international trade transactions to create a smokescreen of legitimacy, obscuring the true intent and source of the funds in a labyrinth of invoices, shipments, and financial dealings.

• The Art of Illusion
Trade-based money laundering involves criminals exploiting the complexities of global trade networks to obfuscate their financial tracks. Like skilled illusionists, they orchestrate a symphony of transactions that appear legitimate on the surface but serve as vehicles for moving tainted wealth across borders.

• The Trojan Horse of Goods
This method lies in the manipulation of goods and services. Criminals overvalue or undervalue merchandise, creating discrepancies between the declared value on invoices and the actual worth. This discrepancy provides a fertile ground for money laundering, as they transfer funds internationally under the guise of legitimate trade transactions.

• The Role of Shell Companies
Shell companies, those enigmatic entities with paper-thin operations, find their place in the world of trade-based money laundering.

Criminals establish these entities in jurisdictions with lax regulations, enabling them to initiate fraudulent trade transactions that amplify the complexity of their web of deceit.

• The Currency Curtain
Criminals adeptly leverage differences in currency exchange rates to further obscure their illicit activities. By exploiting variations in values across markets, they manipulate the perceived value of goods, enabling the movement of funds while leaving investigators chasing phantom paper trails.

• The Networked Deception
This method thrives on networks – networks of shell companies, frontmen, and intermediaries. These intricate relationships form a clandestine ecosystem where fraudulent transactions bounce between entities, making it challenging for law enforcement agencies to trace the flow of funds back to the criminal origin.

• The Regulators' Challenge
Regulators and financial institutions battle to unmask these deceptive practices. Trade-based money laundering poses a formidable challenge due to its complexity and the sheer volume of legitimate trade transactions that occur daily. Enhanced due diligence, risk assessment, and transaction monitoring are among the

tools wielded in the ongoing struggle to detect and prevent these covert activities.

• The Cost of Progress

As global trade advances and evolves, so do the tactics of trade-based money launderers. Cryptocurrencies and digital platforms have presented new opportunities for illicit transactions, demanding that authorities adapt their strategies to confront an ever-changing landscape.

• Navigating the Shadows

Trade-based money laundering stands as a testament to the intricacies of financial deception. While its complex nature presents challenges for both criminals and those tasked with preventing financial crime, the battle against this method continues to underscore the importance of vigilance, collaboration, and innovation in the relentless pursuit of transparency and integrity within the global trade ecosystem.

Bulk Cash Smuggling

The intriguing and clandestine realm of bulk cash smuggling, where criminal networks orchestrate the physical movement of massive amounts of currency across borders with the goal of laundering illicit funds. This practice embodies a fusion of stealth, audacity, and resourcefulness, as criminals navigate international checkpoints, customs regulations, and law enforcement scrutiny in their efforts to cloak the origins of their tainted wealth.

Bulk cash smuggling hinges on the tangible weight of currency. Criminals amass staggering sums through activities such as drug trafficking, extortion, or corruption. Rather than relying on intricate digital transfers, they opt for the physical movement of cash, concealing their wealth within vehicles, containers, or even personal belongings.

The international journey of bulk cash begins with crossing borders. Criminals exploit vulnerabilities at border crossings, airports, and ports to clandestinely move their currency from one jurisdiction to another. By capitalizing on regulatory gaps, they aim to bypass detection and scrutiny.

A Malaysian financier was accused of laundering billions of dollars through real estate investments, including the purchase of luxury properties in the United States and other countries. international banking regulations require financial institutions to report large cash transactions to anti-money laundering authorities. By avoiding these transactions altogether and moving cash in bulk, Jho Low could bypass these regulatory hurdles and keep the origins of the money hidden.

This method hinges on creativity in concealment. Criminals ingeniously stow cash within everyday items, utilizing secret compartments in vehicles, luggage, and even clothing. These hidden compartments become conduits for the transfer of wealth, their very existence a testament to the meticulous planning behind each operation.

Human couriers, sometimes unwittingly, become integral to bulk cash smuggling. Criminals recruit individuals to carry concealed cash across borders, exploiting the difficulty in detecting hidden currency on their persons. These couriers, often coerced or deceived, unwittingly participate in the criminal web of money laundering.

Law enforcement agencies are vigilant in their efforts to curb bulk cash smuggling. Detection techniques range from trained dogs to advanced scanning technology. As authorities refine their strategies, criminals must adapt their methods to circumvent evolving detection methods.

Bulk cash smuggling often intersects with legitimate trade. Criminals manipulate shipments of goods to mask the movement of currency.

By commingling legitimate transactions with illicit activities, they exploit the chaos of global trade networks to their advantage. Bulk cash smuggling thrives on criminal networks and cross-border collaboration. These networks facilitate the logistics of moving currency while leveraging connections within various jurisdictions. The result is a complex web of influence that stretches across borders.

Layering

As we have read earlier the process of money laundering involves three processes and layering is the second one. The process of layering emerges as a pivotal stage where criminals employ a multitude of intricate transactions to obscure the origins of illicit funds. Like an artist layering strokes of paint to create a complex masterpiece, criminals craft a web of financial maneuvers that confound and confuse investigators.

This chapter talks about the art of layering, unveiling the techniques criminals utilize to mask the true source of their ill-gotten gains through a maze of transactions that spans borders, accounts, and financial instruments.

Layering involves a series of convoluted actions that create confusion, complexity, and a seemingly impenetrable trail. Criminals engage in various transactions such as transferring funds between accounts, trading securities, or making fictitious loans. These transactions might occur across multiple jurisdictions, currencies, and financial institutions.By involving numerous intermediaries and incorporating diverse financial instruments, criminals construct a multi-layered veil that obscures the initial connection between the dirty money and its criminal origin.

Teodorin Obiang is the son of Equatorial Guinea's president who faced charges of money laundering and embezzlement, including the acquisition of luxury real estate properties. Teodorin engaged in a web of intricate financial transactions involving shell companies, offshore accounts, and intermediaries. Funds were moved between various entities, both domestic and international, to obfuscate the source of the money.

The primary goal of layering is to distance the illicit funds from their source, making it difficult for authorities to follow the money trail. For instance, a criminal might transfer funds from one account to another, followed by swift exchanges into different currencies.

These funds could then be invested in a shell company that purchases real estate in another country. By the time the funds are reintroduced into the legitimate economy, they have traversed a convoluted path that confounds attempts at tracking their origin.

Layering's complexity is evident in the range of techniques criminals employ. They might engage in high-frequency trading, shifting funds rapidly between stocks and bonds to create a chaotic financial picture. Alternatively, they could simulate international business transactions, generating fabricated invoices that move funds across borders without any actual goods exchanged.

Cryptocurrencies also enter the mix, as criminals convert tainted funds into digital assets that can be transferred quickly and anonymously.

Examples of layering are as diverse as the financial landscape itself. Criminals might exploit online marketplaces, making multiple purchases and returns to create a bewildering sequence of transactions. They could also route funds through a web of intermediaries, utilizing complex loan structures to move money across accounts and jurisdictions. Through these tactics, criminals hope to render the illicit origins of the funds nearly impossible to untangle.We will study the sub division of layering in the upcoming chapters.

Complex Transactions

A puzzle composed of intricate pieces, complex transactions challenge investigators and regulators to untangle the threads of deception that criminals weave within the financial ecosystem.

Complex transactions encompass a wide range of maneuvers that criminals use to confuse and confound. From intricate trade agreements involving multiple parties to the creation of complex financial structures, criminals navigate this intricate landscape with a singular objective: to complicate the money trail beyond easy recognition. By intertwining legitimate transactions with the illicit, criminals create a scenario where discerning the criminal origins of funds becomes an arduous task.

An example of complexity might involve the establishment of a network of shell companies operating across jurisdictions. These entities engage in seemingly legitimate trade transactions, all while funneling illicit funds through convoluted channels. Complex structures can involve layers of intermediaries, offshore accounts, and even legitimate investments, making it challenging to trace the flow of funds to its criminal source.We all know about the famous family of kazakhstan

Members of the influential Kulibayev family in Kazakhstan were accused of laundering money through real estate investments in various countries. Funds were transferred between various accounts, both domestically and internationally. The family used a variety of financial instruments, including stocks, bonds, and investment funds, to create layers of transactions. These layers were designed to confuse investigators by introducing a complex trail of financial activities

Highly intricate financial instruments also come into play. Criminals might engage in swaps, derivatives, or structured products to further obfuscate the money trail. These transactions might involve numerous parties, each contributing to the complexity of the arrangement. Such financial intricacies exploit gaps in regulatory oversight and the complexity of financial instruments to divert attention from the underlying criminal activity.

Cryptocurrencies add a modern twist to the realm of complex transactions. Criminals can utilize digital currencies to create a web of transactions that traverse multiple wallets and exchanges, effectively concealing the movement of funds.

The decentralized nature of cryptocurrencies adds an additional layer of complexity, as tracking transactions across various platforms becomes a significant challenge for investigators.

The evolution of technology and the increasing globalization of financial markets have expanded the toolkit of criminals seeking to execute complex transactions. They exploit these advancements to create a dense forest of transactions, hoping to lose pursuers amidst the trees.

Multiple accounts and jurisdictions

Within the intricate landscape of financial crime, the utilization of multiple accounts and jurisdictions serves as a cornerstone of money laundering. This chapter unveils the complexities inherent in this method, where criminals orchestrate a symphony of financial movements across borders and accounts to obscure the true origins of their tainted wealth. Much like a master chess player maneuvering pieces across a global board, criminals craft a strategic dance that challenges authorities to untangle the intricate threads woven within the vast expanse of the financial world.

Criminals exploit the global nature of financial systems, leveraging multiple jurisdictions to blur the path of their illicit funds. Funds flow seamlessly across borders, moving between accounts situated in different countries. This method capitalizes on variations in regulations and oversight, creating a complex matrix of financial transactions that befuddle investigators.

Multiple accounts serve as nodes in the intricate network criminals create. By distributing funds across various accounts, they create a fragmented landscape that defies straightforward analysis. These accounts can exist within different financial institutions, both domestic and international, adding an additional layer of complexity.

Criminals weave an elaborate web that crisscrosses through numerous accounts and jurisdictions. Funds might be transferred from one account to another, crossing international borders, and even involving intermediaries to further complicate the trail. These transactions might involve the purchase of financial instruments, real estate, or even valuable assets that leave no obvious trace.

Jurisdictions known for their lax financial regulations, often referred to as tax havens or offshore financial centers, become crucial players in this method. Criminals establish accounts and entities in these havens to capitalize on their secrecy provisions, creating an added layer of complexity that hampers investigations.

In the modern age, the digital realm presents new avenues for criminals to exploit multiple accounts and jurisdictions. Cryptocurrencies enable the seamless movement of funds across borders without the traditional banking infrastructure. Criminals can shift between digital wallets and exchanges, concealing their activities in the decentralized landscape of digital currencies.

The stepson of former Malaysian Prime Minister Najib Razak faced money laundering charges related to real estate transactions, including the financing of the film "The Wolf of Wall Street. Riza utilized the international banking system to move funds between these offshore accounts and those in other jurisdictions. Money moved seamlessly across borders, passing through different financial institutions in various countries.

The complexity of money laundering across multiple accounts and jurisdictions presents significant challenges for investigators. Tracing the flow of funds requires international collaboration, navigating intricate legal frameworks, and deciphering the digital intricacies of modern financial transactions.

Fake Transactions

Within the enigmatic realm of financial manipulation, the orchestration of fake transactions emerges as a potent tool for criminals to camouflage the origins of their illicit gains.

This chapter delves into the intricate world of simulated financial activities, where criminals craft a facade of legitimate business dealings to conceal their nefarious intent. Much like skilled magicians wielding sleight of hand, criminals create an illusion of authenticity that bewitches even the most vigilant financial watchdogs.

At the heart of fake transactions lies the creation of transactions that appear real, but are designed solely to obfuscate the flow of tainted funds. Criminals simulate trades, payments, or exchanges that mimic genuine financial activities, blurring the lines between legality and criminality.

Fake trade transactions form a common ploy in this method. Criminals generate invoices, shipping documents, and purchase orders that suggest the movement of goods or services. These documents, often with no physical counterpart, create the illusion of legitimate trade while masking the true purpose of the transactions.

The success of fake transactions lies in their complexity. Criminals choreograph a dance of financial maneuvers that traverse multiple accounts, currencies, and even jurisdictions. By weaving an intricate tapestry of transactions, they confuse auditors and regulators, making it difficult to discern the puppeteer behind the strings.

Criminals employ fictitious debt and loan arrangements to further their ruse. They create false loans or debts between entities, complete with fabricated interest payments and repayment schedules. These transactions introduce a semblance of legitimacy, as they mirror conventional financial activities while masking the true movement of funds.

In the digital age, criminals exploit the speed and anonymity of electronic transactions to amplify the illusion. They fabricate online transactions that appear genuine, routing funds through a labyrinth of digital channels to create a seemingly convoluted trail that resists easy detection.

Fake transactions are not impervious to detection. Financial institutions and regulatory bodies deploy advanced algorithms and artificial intelligence to scrutinize patterns and anomalies. By identifying inconsistencies and anomalies, they aim to expose the counterfeit transactions that underpin money laundering schemes.

International Transactions

Shedding light on how criminals exploit the complexities of cross-border commerce to legitimize illicit funds. In this intricate dance between legitimate trade and criminal intent, criminals leverage the global nature of business to obscure the origins of their tainted wealth. By establishing a facade of legitimate economic activity, they traverse international borders, manipulating financial systems to their advantage while evading detection.

International business transactions provide fertile ground for money laundering due to their inherent complexities. While legitimate businesses engage in cross-border trade to expand markets and foster economic growth, criminals infiltrate this system to legitimize their ill-gotten gains. This dual nature of commerce becomes a veil behind which criminals operate, leveraging legitimate transactions to mask their true intent.

The complexity of international business transactions serves as a smokescreen for money laundering. Criminals manipulate invoices, shipping documents, and financial statements to create an illusion of legitimate trade. This complexity thwarts efforts to trace the flow of funds, as they become entangled within the intricate web of global commerce.

Criminals exploit the valuation of goods to launder money. Overvaluation and undervaluation of traded goods provide opportunities for criminals to manipulate the perceived value of transactions. Overvaluing goods can facilitate the transfer of funds across borders, while undervaluing them can lead to an influx of seemingly legitimate funds that blend with genuine economic activity.

Trade-based money laundering emerges as a distinct method within international business transactions. Criminals manipulate invoices, fictitious shipments, and fabricated trade deals to move funds across borders while camouflaging the illicit origins. These maneuvers exploit the complexity of trade networks, leveraging legitimate trade flows to obscure criminal activities.

The digital era amplifies the potential for international business-related money laundering. Cryptocurrencies facilitate cross-border transactions without traditional banking channels, allowing criminals to move funds seamlessly across borders. This digital globalization creates new challenges for authorities striving to monitor and regulate international financial flows.

Nominee and front companies

The utilization of nominees and front companies emerges as a critical tactic for criminals seeking to obscure their true identities and the origins of their illicit wealth. This chapter delves into the shadowy realm where criminals orchestrate a symphony of actors and entities to operate in their stead, casting a web of illusion that challenges investigators and regulators to unveil the hidden faces behind the financial curtain.

Nominees and front companies act as proxies, masking the true beneficiaries of financial transactions. Criminals enlist individuals or entities to hold and manage assets on their behalf, effectively distancing themselves from the illicit funds. This proxy arrangement introduces a layer of complexity that hampers efforts to trace the flow of money.

Front companies, often established as paper entities, play a central role in money laundering schemes. Criminals set up these companies to engage in seemingly legitimate business activities, providing a cloak of authenticity to their operations. These entities become conduits through which illicit funds flow, confounding attempts to identify the true source of wealth.

Nominee directors and shareholders lend their identities to facilitate money laundering. Criminals appoint individuals as nominal directors or shareholders of companies, granting them apparent control over these entities. In reality, these nominees merely follow instructions from the true beneficiaries, masking their involvement and intentions.

The international nature of nominees and front companies amplifies their effectiveness. Criminals exploit differences in jurisdictional regulations to establish these entities in locations with weak oversight. This international maze hinders investigators, as the true beneficiaries traverse borders, rendering the pursuit of justice more complex.

Nominees and front companies obscure the true ownership of assets. By placing assets under the names of proxies, criminals thwart attempts to identify their involvement. This strategic maneuver makes it challenging to follow the money trail and uncover the criminal origins of funds.

The recognition that while the utilization of nominees and front companies stands as a testament to the intricate layers of money laundering, it also underscores the resilience of financial institutions, law enforcement agencies, and regulators who strive to reveal the true actors behind the façade and maintain the integrity of the financial system.

Swapping currencies

The method of currency swapping emerges as a clever maneuver employed by criminals to obscure the origins of their ill-gotten gains. This chapter delves into the world of deceptive currency exchanges, where criminals exploit the volatility and complexity of global currency markets to mask the flow of tainted funds. Much like master illusionists, they orchestrate a delicate dance between currencies, creating a smokescreen that challenges authorities to trace the origins of the hidden wealth.

Currency markets, known for their rapid fluctuations, provide an ideal cover for money laundering. Criminals leverage these fluctuations to shuffle funds between different currencies, exploiting the inherent complexity to muddy the money trail. Currency swapping introduces a layer of confusion that obscures the true origins of the illicit wealth.

Currency swapping involves orchestrated trades between two different currencies. Criminals execute these trades in a manner that mimics legitimate trading activities. These transactions could involve buying and selling large volumes of currency pairs, creating a façade of active participation in the global currency market.

The international nature of currency markets adds to the complexity of this method. Criminals capitalize on the ease of transferring funds across borders, often exploiting multiple jurisdictions to further complicate the tracking process. By traversing borders, they exploit varying regulatory landscapes, making detection a formidable challenge.

Currency swapping enables criminals to distance themselves from the original source of funds. As tainted funds are exchanged between currencies, the connection between the illicit activities and the resulting transactions becomes increasingly obscure. This method of obfuscation thwarts attempts to uncover the true origins of the funds.

Criminals leverage electronic trading platforms to execute currency swaps. These platforms allow them to execute transactions quickly and anonymously, further enhancing the illusion of legitimate trading. Digital currencies add a layer of complexity, as they can be easily converted and moved across borders.

Currency swapping requires a deep understanding of currency markets and trading strategies. Criminals often employ financial experts who can execute these transactions with precision, avoiding suspicion and maintaining the illusion of legitimate trading activities

Trade Mispricing

World of deceptive trade activities, where criminals exploit the complexities of international trade to create a facade of legitimate commerce while channeling tainted funds across borders. Much like master weavers crafting intricate patterns, they orchestrate transactions that challenge investigators to discern the true value and intent behind the trades.

Trade mispricing involves manipulating the value of goods or services traded across borders. Criminals intentionally overvalue or undervalue these transactions to create an appearance of legitimate trade activities. By distorting the prices, they generate a smokescreen that conceals the movement of illicit funds within the legitimate flow of commerce.

Criminals employ two main tactics within trade mispricing: overvaluation and undervaluation. Overvaluation inflates the value of goods or services, allowing criminals to move excessive funds across borders. Undervaluation, on the other hand, understates the value, enabling them to inject illicit funds into the financial system without raising suspicions.

International trade involves a complex web of transactions, documentation, and participants. Criminals leverage this complexity to their advantage, orchestrating intricate networks of companies, intermediaries, and financial institutions. By weaving a tangled web of transactions, they create confusion that obscures the true intent of their activities.

Shell companies and intermediaries play a pivotal role in trade mispricing schemes. Criminals establish these entities in various jurisdictions, using them as conduits to manipulate prices and move funds. The layers of complexity these entities introduce make it challenging for investigators to trace the movement of funds back to their criminal origin.

Trade mispricing effectively camouflages illicit financial flows within the legitimate trade system. Criminals divert funds through the overpriced or underpriced transactions, making the money trail appear as part of the routine ebb and flow of global commerce. This method blurs the line between legitimate trade and money laundering.

The method of trade mispricing emerges as a cunning maneuver employed by criminals to obscure the origins of their illicit wealth.

Now the practices involved in layering are done so we will understand the last part of money laundering, the integration .

Integration

Reintegration into the legitimate economy is the pivotal final stage of the money laundering process, where illicitly acquired funds are seamlessly merged with lawful financial activities, effectively obscuring their origins and presenting them as legitimate assets. This phase is the ultimate goal for money launderers, as it allows them to enjoy the ill-gotten gains without raising suspicions or attracting the attention of authorities. Reintegration involves complex financial maneuvers and transactions that facilitate the transition from "dirty" money to "clean" assets, making it exceedingly challenging for law enforcement and financial institutions to trace the illicit funds back to their criminal source.

During the earlier stages of money laundering, namely placement and layering, criminals employ strategies to distance themselves from the illicit funds and create a complex web of transactions to obfuscate the trail. Reintegration serves as the culmination of these efforts, where the laundered funds are made to seamlessly blend into the legitimate economic landscape. This can be achieved through various means, each exploiting the intricacies of financial systems, global trade, and investments.

One common method of reintegration involves investing the laundered funds into legitimate businesses. By acquiring or investing in established companies, criminals not only infuse the illicit funds into a lawful economic activity but also gain the opportunity to earn legitimate profits. These profits become commingled with the genuine earnings of the business, making it challenging to discern the illicit origins.

Real estate transactions also serve as a popular avenue for reintegration. Criminals may use laundered funds to purchase properties, which can then be leased or sold. The income generated from these properties appears legitimate, as it stems from rent or property appreciation. These assets can be further leveraged to obtain loans or mortgages, perpetuating the illusion of legality.

Financial markets provide another avenue for reintegration. Criminals might invest the laundered funds in stocks, bonds, or other financial instruments. These investments generate returns that, on the surface, seem legitimate and can be reinvested or withdrawn without raising suspicions. The complexity of global financial systems and the anonymity offered by certain financial instruments contribute to the challenges of identifying illicit flows.

The digital age has introduced new dimensions to reintegration, with cryptocurrencies offering an additional layer of anonymity and complexity. Criminals can convert laundered funds into cryptocurrencies and execute transactions that span international borders with relative ease. This digital reintegration further complicates the whole.

Reintegration into the legitimate economy is the culmination of the money laundering process, where criminals employ intricate methods to seamlessly merge their ill-gotten gains with lawful economic activities. Whether through investments in businesses, real estate, financial instruments, or digital currencies, criminals strive to erase any traces of their criminal origins and enjoy the benefits of their illicit activities. The complexity of reintegration methods underscores the ongoing challenges faced by authorities in their efforts to maintain the integrity of the global financial system and combat money laundering.

Investment in Businesses

Criminals leverage this avenue to seamlessly integrate illicit funds into the legitimate economy, blurring the lines between criminal activities and lawful financial operations. By orchestrating investments in businesses, they craft a façade of legitimacy that masks the origins of their ill-gotten gains, challenging authorities to discern the true nature of these financial transactions.

Investment in businesses serves as an effective means for criminals to launder money. They strategically inject laundered funds into existing companies or startups, seeking to capitalize on the potential for growth and profit. This infusion of illicit capital creates an appearance of financial health, concealing the criminal source behind a veneer of legitimate economic activity.

Criminals employ various strategies to invest in businesses. They might establish their own entities to funnel illicit funds or acquire ownership stakes in existing companies. These investments can take the form of equity ownership, debt instruments, or convertible securities, each presenting an opportunity to blend tainted money with lawful financial transactions.

The integration of illicit funds through business investments aims to obscure the origins of the money. By mingling the laundered funds with genuine investments and earnings, criminals create a financial landscape that thwarts efforts to trace back to their illegal activities.

This complexity challenges regulatory bodies and law enforcement agencies tasked with maintaining financial transparency.

Investments in businesses generate returns that can further distance the funds from their illicit origins. Criminals capitalize on these returns to legitimize the gains. Dividends, interest payments, or capital appreciation become intertwined with legitimate financial operations, making it difficult to discern the presence of illicit funds within the financial ecosystem.

Business investments offer criminals a diverse array of opportunities for money laundering. They might invest in industries spanning from technology to real estate, diversifying their holdings and evading detection through the breadth of their ventures. This multidimensional approach amplifies the challenge of uncovering the criminal thread within the legitimate business fabric.

Detecting money laundering through business investments requires vigilance and collaboration. Financial institutions must enhance due diligence practices to identify unusual patterns or sources of funds.

Real Estate Holdings

Effectively transforming tainted money into seemingly legitimate assets. Like architects constructing a façade, money launderers orchestrate these transactions to obscure the origins of their wealth, presenting a significant challenge to authorities aiming to unravel the complex web of deceit.

• The Foundations of Concealment
Real estate investments provide a solid foundation for money launderers to hide illicit funds. Criminals purchase residential or commercial properties, using them as repositories for their tainted wealth. These assets not only retain their value but often appreciate over time, offering a means to legitimize the proceeds of criminal activities.

• The Mechanisms of Acquisition
Criminals employ various methods to acquire real estate holdings. They may use shell companies or nominees to purchase properties, concealing their true ownership. These transactions can involve cash purchases, complicating efforts to trace the source of funds. Additionally, money launderers may invest in luxury properties or properties in high-demand markets to further obfuscate their activities.

• The Veil of Legitimacy

Real estate holdings serve as a mask that conceals the origins of illicit funds. Criminals rent or lease properties, generating rental income that appears legitimate. Alternatively, they may sell properties, effectively converting laundered funds into clean, legal assets. This complex web of real estate transactions camouflages the criminal trail within the legitimate property market.

• The Global Landscape

The international nature of real estate markets adds to the complexity of money laundering through property holdings. Criminals often purchase properties in foreign countries, taking advantage of differing regulations and tax environments. This international dimension makes it challenging for authorities to track and investigate these transactions effectively.

• Concealing Ownership

Real estate transactions allow criminals to hide behind layers of ownership and legal structures. Shell companies, trusts, and offshore entities frequently serve as vehicles for concealing the true beneficiaries of property holdings. These layers of complexity stymie efforts to identify the individuals behind the illicit wealth.

Charitable Donations

While charitable giving is a noble endeavor, it can be exploited by criminals seeking to legitimize their illicit funds. Like philanthropists with hidden agendas, money launderers orchestrate donations to charitable organizations, concealing the true source of their wealth behind a veil of altruism. This practice poses a unique challenge for authorities striving to uphold the integrity of the nonprofit sector while detecting and deterring money laundering.

Charitable donations offer money launderers a veneer of legitimacy. Criminals channel their tainted funds into nonprofit organizations, making it appear as though they are supporting charitable causes. This not only obscures the illicit source of the funds but also grants them a potential tax benefit, further complicating the detection process.

Criminals employ various methods to execute charitable donations. They may establish their own charitable foundations or trusts, effectively controlling the funds while maintaining a guise of benevolence. Alternatively, they can make direct donations to existing nonprofits, often using intermediaries or nominees to further obscure their involvement.

The nonprofit sector is vast and diverse, offering numerous opportunities for money laundering. Criminals may target charitable organizations with legitimate missions, using their infrastructure to legitimize their donations. Additionally, they may exploit the lack of transparency in some charitable sectors, making it challenging for authorities to scrutinize the financial flows.

Charitable donations can confer tax advantages, which criminals exploit to their benefit. By making substantial donations to nonprofits, they not only cleanse their funds but also reduce their tax liability. This intersection of money laundering and tax evasion adds an additional layer of complexity to the process.

Detecting money laundering through charitable donations requires a delicate balance between preserving the nonprofit sector's integrity and preventing illicit financial activities.

End Note

As we conclude this exploration of the multifaceted world of money laundering, it becomes evident that financial deception is an intricate dance, where criminals craft elaborate schemes to hide the origins of their illicit wealth. From the placement of tainted funds into the financial system to their layering through complex transactions and ultimately their integration into legitimate assets, money launderers employ a vast array of strategies.

Throughout this journey, we've witnessed criminals harness the global nature of finance, exploiting the complexities of international trade, real estate, investments, and even charitable donations. They have adeptly used financial instruments, offshore accounts, and digital currencies to obfuscate their trails, often transcending borders and jurisdictions. In doing so, they challenge the very foundations of financial integrity.

However, in the face of these challenges, we've also observed the resilience of regulatory bodies, financial institutions, law enforcement agencies, and international cooperation. Their tireless efforts to enhance due diligence practices, promote transparency, and adapt to evolving financial landscapes stand as a testament to the commitment to thwarting financial crime.

This book's journey through the phases of money laundering, from the initial placement of funds to their integration into the legitimate economy, has shed light on the intricate tactics employed by criminals. It underscores the need for vigilance, innovation, and global collaboration in the ongoing battle against money laundering.

As we look to the future, we must remain vigilant, continually adapting to emerging threats and evolving technologies. The fight against money laundering is a collective endeavor that transcends borders, industries, and disciplines. It demands unwavering commitment from governments, financial institutions, nonprofits, and individuals alike.

In the relentless pursuit of financial transparency and accountability, we unveil the shadows that conceal illicit wealth. By exposing the intricate layers of money laundering and sharing knowledge, we strengthen our collective ability to detect, deter, and ultimately dismantle the complex networks that facilitate financial crime.

In the pages of this book, we've embarked on a journey through the intricate world of taxes, tax optimization, and the transformation of "black money" into "white money." Our exploration has unveiled the strategies, motivations, and consequences that underlie these practices. We've navigated through the complexities of tax laws, ethical considerations, and the societal impacts of financial decisions.

As we conclude this journey, it is imperative to underscore the importance of responsible financial citizenship. The choices individuals and businesses make regarding taxes reverberate far beyond balance sheets. They shape economies, influence public services, and determine the quality of life for countless people.

Our understanding of "black money" and its transformation into "white money" should prompt us to reflect on the moral and ethical dimensions of our financial decisions. Responsible tax practices are not merely legal obligations; they are ethical imperatives. We are all stakeholders in the social contract, and our contributions, in the form of taxes, are the lifeblood of our societies.

We must advocate for transparency, fairness, and accountability in financial dealings. Governments must continue to strengthen regulations and close loopholes to ensure that tax systems are just and equitable. Businesses, as corporate citizens, should uphold ethical standards that prioritize social responsibility alongside profitability.

This book serves as a reminder that while tax optimization is a legitimate endeavor, it should always align with the broader goal of fostering prosperous and equitable societies. We all share a responsibility to contribute our fair share to support public goods, such as education, healthcare, infrastructure, and social safety nets. These investments are the foundation of vibrant, inclusive communities.

In the end, our financial decisions should reflect a commitment to the common good. Let us navigate the world of finance not only with an eye on the bottom line but with a vision of a more just and compassionate world. It is through our collective efforts as responsible financial citizens that we can build societies where prosperity is shared, opportunities are accessible to all, and the promise of a better future is realized.

www.ingramcontent.com/pod-product-compliance
Lightning Source LLC
Chambersburg PA
CBHW072205290526
45794CB00004B/1658